Healing Methods: An Overview

By Rev. Dr. Angela Plum, Ph.D
Minister of Spiritual Science
Spiritual Healer
Registered Polarity Practitioner
Certified Zero Balancer

Publisher: Ralph Roberts

Executive Editor: Kathryn L. Hall

Cover Design: WorldComm®

Interior Design and Typesetting: WorldComm®

Printed in the United States of America

10 9 8 7 6 5 4 3 2 1

ISBN 1-56664-051-2

Library of Congress Catalog Card Number:

WorldComm—a Division of Creativity, Inc., 65 Macedonia Road, Alexander, North Carolina 28701, (704) 252-9515—is a full-service publisher.

Trademarks
Names of products that are suspected of being trademarks or service marks are capitalized. Use of a product or service name in this book should not be regarded as affecting the validity of any trademark or service mark.

This book reflects the personal experience of the author and does not exclude standard medical care. See your physician and use alternative methods to stay healthy.

This book is dedicated to all my healing teachers, both those on the physical plane and those in spirit.

Acknowledgments

I wish to thank the following people and organizations for their permission to use material.

The National Federation of Spiritual Healers of America, Inc. for permission to use their logo on the front cover.

The American Polarity Therapy Association for their encouragement and advice.

Fritz Smith, M.D. for his editing and comments on the Zero Balancing chapter.

Aminah Raheem, PhD. for permission to mention her books.

Iona Marsaa Teeguarden for permission to use her chart on "Basic Neck and Shoulder Release" in the Acupressure chapter.

Alternate Healing Methods: An Overview

Contents

ALTERNATE HEALING METHODS:
AN OVERVIEW

CHAPTER 1

The Beginning

This book was developed in response to questions by many people. They wanted to know either how to be a healer or how the healing process operates. Through the years, I have studied many healing modalities and met some of the best healers and teachers in the world. There are likely as many healing methods as there are healers. You may have experience with methods unknown to me. I can only share my personal experiences and methods with you. This I will attempt to do in the following pages.

Let us start at the beginning. I had a "death experience" in 1950 which awakened in me a great desire to help others. The first of my five children was born at that time so I was very busy with the daily involvement of their care for the next 13 years. However, during those years I read constantly, studying the holy books of all the major religions and developing a very strong personal relationship with God. In those holy books I found a string of truth that connected the major religions. In them also were stories of miracles. It seemed that unconditional love was the common denominator. So I strived to develop unconditional love toward all I encountered, asking for God's guidance every day.

During the years that my children were small, they had many illnesses and accidents, as small children are prone to have. In addition to the medical help of a wonderful family doctor, I asked God to send healing to them. At that time I did not realize that human beings could be transmitters of healing energies but, after praying, whenever I touched someone needing healing, they felt better.

My doctor was impressed with the fast recovery of my children and showed me first aid techniques and even how to cut adhesive tape to use in place of sutures for cuts. (This was prior to the manufacture of butterfly bandages.) After that I rarely had to take them to the emergency room for stitches. Even neighborhood children were brought to me to "fix" when they were injured. This all seemed very natural. It was many years later before I understood how the transmission of healing energies occurred. I then realized that I had been able to tap into this energy.

Healers will tell you that they do not do the healing. They have to get their ego out of the way and let God's energy come through them. This is one of the most difficult things to learn to do. We always want to be in control and fear a loss of this control. By learning how to "let go and let God" do it, we become open channels for God's healing grace. A by-product of being a channel is that we get healed by the healing energy that comes through us just as surely as the water pipe gets wet when the water comes through it.

When I look back at my life, I can see how I was guided to read certain books, to meet certain people, to attend conferences, and to study different healing methods. I have been privileged to meet and study with some of the best psychics, teachers, and healers in the world. In chapter 2, I will relate the chronology of these events.

The Journey Continues

In 1963 I was introduced to Spiritual Frontiers Fellowship (SFF). This is an organization dedicated to examining psychic phenomena through the established churches. They presented local lectures and workshops and had annual conferences at college campuses. These conferences usually lasted a week and had classes on parapsychology and healing, lectures by world-known experts in the field, and appointments available with psychics and healers.

Through the local SFF organization in Baltimore, Maryland, I met Olga and Ambrose Worrall, the great healers. (You can read about them in their book, **"THE GIFT OF HEALING".**) They had weekly healing services at their "New Life Clinic" at Mt. Washington Methodist Church. I attended many of their lectures and services. Olga continued her activity after Ambrose's death both at the "New Life Clinic" and at SFF conferences. They were both a great inspiration to me.

By 1969, I had met eight other people who also had psychic or spiritual experiences. It was so wonderful to find others to talk with who would understand the life-changing effects of these experiences. We began meeting on a weekly basis, having discussions and meditations. We studied everything we could find, including astrology, numerology, Theosophy, telepathy, psychometry, color therapy, kinesiology, Alice Bailey and Edgar Cayce material. At this time I made a personal commitment to God to do His work and be of service to humanity.

In 1970, I attended a conference given by SFF at Gettysburg College in Pennsylvania. I had three psychic readings and at each one the psychic told me I was a healer. When I asked how to heal, each told me it was an individual thing, so I had to develop my own channel. Needless to say, this became very frustrating. There was a wonderful healer from England who was teaching at the conference. Gordon Turner was responsible for getting the British Parliament to change the laws to allow spiritual healers to go into hospitals and clinics and to have private healing practices. I was very impressed with

Gordon. In 1971, I again attended the SFF conference at Gettysburg College, and Gordon Turner was there. After a year of frustration and trying to figure out how to become a healer I made an appointment to see Gordon, who was giving private healing sessions. He required each person to meditate for 15 minutes before being seen, so I did this. When Gordon came into the room, he looked at me and said, "There is not much wrong with you, but you want to know how to heal." It amazed me that he knew this since most people saw him to obtain healing. Anyway, I replied that, indeed, I wanted to know how to be a healer.

Gordon told me that it was true that each person must develop their own channel, but he would show me how he healed. He sat me in a chair, stood behind me and placed his hands on my shoulders. He said, "I make a three-fold attunement; to the God above, the God within me, and the God within the person asking for healing. When the attunement is made, healing always occurs." As Gordon made this attunement, I felt an energy come from his hands that was so strong that it felt as if he was beating on my shoulders although his hands did not physically move. I was filled with awe as if in the Presence of God. All my minor pains were removed and I felt vitalized. Gordon removed his hands, then sat and talked with me. He told me to "practice, practice, practice" the laying-on-of-hands whenever there was an opportunity to do so. He said that by doing this I would develop a channel for the transmission of healing energies.

When I returned home from the conference, I asked my meditation group to start having a weekly healing circle at the meetings. They agreed to this, so after our meditation we placed a chair in the center of the circle of people and took turns sitting in the chair. As Gordon Turner had instructed, I told them how to make the three-fold attunement. Then, using my inner guidance, I explained how to channel energy (see chapter 3). Pretty soon we were getting led to place our hands on the place needing healing without being told the problem. We became much more in touch with our inner guidance. As each of us had our turn sitting in the chair and receiving the laying-on-of-hands of the others, we felt energized and balanced.

It was nine months later that a significant change occurred. As we were doing the healing circle, placing our hands on one member, I suddenly felt like I was plugged into an electric socket. Tremendous energy flowed through me and out of my hands.

The person in the chair was relieved of a chronic health problem of many years' duration. Then I knew that all of the practicing had worked. I had opened a channel for the transmission of healing energies. Even the fact that it took nine months seemed significant, since it also takes nine months for children to develop from conception to term.

This perfect attunement and tremendous flow of energy does not happen often. When it does, there is instantaneous healing and what we call a "miracle" occurs. I believe that a miracle is really a natural occurrence that just needs a perfect three-fold attunement to bring the proper vibratory frequency for health. Everything is vibration. Discordant vibration is dis-ease. If we bring the discordant vibration into harmony and balance by the transmission of healing energies, the dis-ease is removed and health restored. By keeping our energies balanced, we stay healthy.

We continued the healing circle weekly in the meditation group. By 1972, group members were bringing family and friends to receive the laying-on-of-hands. Also, in 1972 I began a correspondence course in spiritual healing from the **NATIONAL FEDERATION OF SPIRITUAL HEALERS** in England. Gordon Turner had helped establish that organization.

In 1974, I attended a class in "Psychic Acupuncture" taught by Etel DeLoach at the SFF conference at Elizabethtown College in Pennsylvania. This is another method of channeling God's energy. At that same conference my friend, Helen Potter, had picked up a book titled **"WE ARE ALL HEALERS"** by Sally Hammond. The book kept opening to the page that told about Madame Takata, the world's last remaining Reiki master after World War II. I was very impressed with the information given about Takata and Reiki, so I told Helen that we were going to study Reiki even if we had to go to Hawaii to do it. However, Helen wrote to Takata and invited her to come to Baltimore to teach us Reiki. Takata came in August 1976 and taught Reiki to 48 people. In 1976 I also took a weekend workshop on "Psychic Surgery" given by Dr. Raymond Reed.

Beginning in August 1976, I invited Reiki healers to my house to practice Reiki on a weekly basis. At first we worked on each other, then people began to ask for healing work by the group. Soon we had to set up appointments in order to handle the volume of requests. In 1976 I also traveled to England and studied with British healers at Stanstead Hall.

After I finished the healing course with

the **NATIONAL FEDERATION OF SPIRI-TUAL HEALERS,** I continued my studies. I was initiated as an I.A. (Integrated Awareness) graduate in September 1977 and studied "Psychic Diagnosis" in April 1978. Both of these courses were taught by Consuelo Newton and increased my ability to be aware of inner guidance.

Ethel Lombardi had been made a Reiki master by Takata. When Takata retired, Ethel came to Baltimore in 1978 and initiated us into Reiki II. The Reiki group kept working weekly so there was a place for each new class of Reiki healers to practice until they became comfortable with being on their own.

In 1979 I studied "Spiritual Healing" with Margie Woods, who had studied with the Philippine psychic surgeons, and I studied color therapy with both Georgina Regan and Theo Gimbel (Queen Elizabeth's color therapist). In 1981 I studied "Body Electronics" with John Ray.

Year after year, as I worked with the Reiki group, my inner guidance became stronger. I was impressed to place my hands in positions that were not the Reiki positions but they worked to balance the body energies. Then I discovered that some of those positions were used in Polarity Therapy which was an energy-balancing method developed by Dr. Randolph Stone. I needed to intellectually understand how and why the hand positions worked so, beginning in 1982, I traveled to Bethesda, Maryland, for two years and studied Polarity Therapy with Chloe Wadsworth who had been a student of Dr. Stone's. I began a private energy-balancing practice in order to use the different methods of healing. I was still studying Polarity Therapy when I discovered that some of the other hand positions that my guidance led me to use were also used in Zero Balancing (ZB). ZB is an energy-balancing method developed by a medical doctor, Fritz Frederick Smith, who lived in California. So, again needing to intellectually understand how the method worked, I called Dr. Smith and arranged to study with him.

While studying Polarity Therapy and Zero Balancing I also became a Healing Practitioner through Rev. Carol Parrish's **LIGHT OF CHRIST COMMUNITY CHURCH (Tahlequah, Oklahoma)** and a MariEl healer. Ethel Lombardi had prayed for a faster method of healing and, what was given to her, she called MariEl. So in 1983 Ethel came to Baltimore and taught us MariEl. Then the Reiki group became a MariEl group and continued to function weekly. Meanwhile, after being certified in Polarity and ZB, I continued taking post-graduate courses including Craniosacral Therapy and Reflexology. In 1985, I purchased a magnetic field machine from Switzerland and included magnetic therapy in my private practice.

In 1988, Alberto Aguas, the Brazilian healer, came to my home and taught a method of healing that he had learned in the Amazon jungles from the Guaranis Indians. He called the method, Ama Deus, meaning "I love God." Included in this method of healing are excellent techniques in absent healing and ways to help dying persons.

Even though I had studied many healing techniques and was certified in them, something was missing. I needed to have the spiritual side of healing recognized, so I began studying for the ministry and entered **THE INTERNATIONAL COLLEGE OF SPIRITUAL AND PSYCHIC SCIENCES**. My dream was fulfilled in May 1990 when I was ordained in Montreal by the Reverend Marilyn Rossner as a minister of Spiritual Science. That summer I also became a founding member of the **NATIONAL FEDERATION OF SPIRITUAL HEALERS OF AMERICA, INC.** and was recognized by them as a Spiritual Healer. My studies at the International College continued as I earned a Masters in Ministry and my book **"AN INTERFAITH MINISTER'S MANUAL"** became my doctoral thesis. In 1993 I earned a Ph.D.

I will always continue to learn new methods. However, I have found that the journey has come full circle. In the beginning, I just listened to my inner guidance as to where to place my hands to channel healing energies. Then, because I am an intellectual person also, I needed to learn how and why different methods of healing worked. Now, after studying for over 20 years, I have come back to just listening to my inner guidance. It is true that each person must develop their own channel, but I do not want you to be as frustrated as I was when I was told this in 1970. So I have written this book to give you insight into different healing methods.

CHAPTER 3

How to Channel Energy

There are steps you can take to become a healing channel. They are:

1. Have the intention to be of service.
2. Contact the Divine Essence within by meditating daily.
3. Practice the laying-on-of-hands to develop a channel for the healing energies.

The most important step is your intention to be of service. After stating your intention, get in touch with your inner guidance by devoting a small portion to your day to meditation.

How do you meditate? One how-to book I can recommend is titled **"HOW TO MEDITATE, A GUIDE TO SELF-DISCOVERY"** by Lawrence LeShan (Ballantine paperback, 1975). LeShan describes meditating as "a discipline that trains the personality and brings more efficiency and serenity." Meditation also helps develop an ability to use other modes of being. It is in this other mode of being, or altered state, that we can be channels of healing energies.

A simple, easy way to meditate is simply to sit with your spine straight, and hands and feet uncrossed. Just silently count the length of your inbreath and the length of your outbreath until they are the same length. This only takes a minute or two. When the breath is evenly balanced, all the body systems have slowed and relaxed, and your brain waves are entering the alpha wave state. It is in the alpha state that you can get in touch with the Divine Essence within your being. It need only take five minutes, or better yet, just think inwardly for a minute each hour or several times a day.

Finally, as Gordon Turner told me, practice, practice, practice being a channel. If you have friends who are willing to work with you, start a weekly healing circle. If you cannot do this, practice on your family and pets any chance you can.

The Law of Cure

It is helpful for you to understand and be able to explain the Law of Cure to the person receiving healing in case of a recurrence of their symptoms. There can be instantaneous healing when a perfect attunement is made but, unfortunately, this is rare.

The normal reaction is a gradual improvement of the problem over time. The natural Law of Cure is:

- Healing occurs from the inside to the outside. There will be improvements in attitudes and feelings before physical symptoms change. (Healing also takes place on an upward spiral, usually reaching its peak three days after the initial healing session. It would thus be advantageous to schedule another healing session in a week.)

- Healing moves from the top downward or from head to foot. Example: A rash will start clearing from the top of the body first.

- Symptoms will reappear and clear in the opposite order that they appeared, so recently occurring conditions respond more quickly than chronic conditions. (All disease or discordant energy that has lodged in the cellular memory of the body must be released in order to be cured. When these symptoms are experienced after a healing session, it is called a "healing crisis" and will last a very short time. However, it is a good sign that the problem has been eliminated.)

There are many methods of channelling energy. The rest of this book is a survey course, an overview, of some of the healing methods I have personally experienced.

CHAPTER 4

Spiritual Healing

There is a difference between "Faith Healing" and "Spiritual Healing." In "Faith Healing," the person asking for healing must have faith that something will occur. In "Spiritual Healing," God's energy is channelled to the person whether they have faith or not. They just have to be open to the possibility and not block the flow of energy by being set against it.

Begin by making the three-fold attunement: (1) to the God above; (2) to the God within you; and (3) to the God within the person needing healing. Visualize God's white light coming down from infinity, flowing through the top of your head, into your heart, and connecting with the God Essence within you. Breathe in deeply and **FEEL** the energy coming in. Then breathe out and **FEEL** the energy coming from your heart and out of your hands. When the energy is flowing well, place them on the person needing healing. Ask for guidance as to where to place your hands and what to do for the highest good of the person requesting healing. Listen within for inspiration. **LET GO AND LET GOD** send the healing energies through you. Get out of the way. That is all that is needed. There is an intelligence in every atom of the body that will respond to the God-given energy.

Absent Healing

You can be a channel for God's healing energy without being present with the sick person. There is no barrier (either time or space) as we exist in an Eternal Now. Sit quietly, breathe deeply and evenly, and get in tune with the Divine Essence within you. Visualize the person needing healing as standing in front of you. See them as whole, healthy, and happy. (Even if the person is missing a limb, see them as being whole.) Make the three-fold attunement and visualize the Divine Light or energy coming down from God through the top of your head and into your heart. **FEEL** the connection. When you feel the energy, send it out from your heart to the heart of the person needing healing. **SEE AND FEEL** the Divine Energy filling and surrounding the person with light.

You only need to hold the image long enough to see this. It may only take 15 seconds or so. Release the image and relax. Forget about it. It is done.

If you are asked to pray for healing for a sick person but you do not know what they look like, you can do this. Get in touch with the Divine Essence within you. Bring in the Divine Energy. Then **WRITE THE NAME OF THE PERSON IN LIGHT.** Simply act "as if" you had a laser beam of light in your finger and write the name. If the soul of that person wants healing, they will get it.

Be careful who you ask to pray for you. If the person does not understand about creating with thought and emotion, they can make you worse. We must **ALWAYS** visualize a person as whole when asking for healing (or praying) for them.

The Power of Thought

THIS IS ONE OF THE MOST IMPORTANT PIECES OF INFORMATION YOU WILL EVER LEARN.

God made us co-creators. We create by having a clear mental image and putting emotion to it to power or bring it into physical manifestation. People cause the problems in their lives by thinking negative thoughts and having the fear that these negative situations will occur. By doing this, they actually bring the situation they fear into their lives. This is what worry does.

DO NOT WORRY. Whenever you have a negative thought, stop at once and do not put an emotion to it. (A thought that is not powered by an emotion will dissipate like smoke.) Cancel the negative thought by replacing it with a thought of the positive situation you want and bring that into your life by **DESIRING** it. Remember we create by a clear thought with an emotion. Watch your thoughts. Begin a new habit of paying attention to your thoughts and only allowing positive ones to have the energy of emotion. This will change your life.

The National Federation of Spiritual Healers of America, Inc.

This is an organization dedicated to supporting spiritual healers and those interested in healing. It was founded by Nancy Love and Peter Greene. The work of NFSHA includes networking, newsletters, conferences, training programs, seminars for development, and conducting research. In 1993, NFSHA sponsored conferences in Orlando, FL; Atlanta, GA; Houston, TX; Asheville, NC; and San Francisco, CA.

NFSHA has been represented at a conference sponsored by the National Institute of Health, which has received a $2 million congressional appropriation to do research into alternative healing methods. NIH has established an Office For The Study of Unconventional Medicine.

To join NFSHA or obtain information on spiritual healers in your area or on the conferences, write to:

> **NFSHA**
> P.O. Box 2022,
> Mt. Pleasant, SC 29465
>
> or call Nancy Love at (803) 849-1529.

CHAPTER 5

Reiki

Reiki (ray key) is a Japanese word meaning "Universal Life Energy." The Reiki system is Zen Buddhist and is over 2500 years old. It works by channelling energy from a higher source through the healer's hands into the body of another or oneself. After being "attuned" to channel the universal life force, techniques are taught for placement of the hands on all the vital spots on the body that relate to the organs. The body draws the energy it needs, which is usually felt as unusual heat or coolness or a tingling sensation. A treatment usually lasts about an hour. Reiki heals the cause of illness and eliminates the effect.

Reiki is not a religion, although it is very spiritual. It is a LOVE VIBRATION which restores harmony. It was discovered by Dr. Mikao Usui who was President of the Christian University in Kyoto, Japan in the late

1800s. During a sermon, Dr. Usui was challenged to do the miracles the Bible tells of and not just accept it on faith. Some young men about to graduate insisted they would believe in the Bible only if they could be shown it was possible for people to do what was said there. Dr. Usui admitted he could not be a living example of the teachings, so he resigned his position as a minister. He came to the United States, a Christian country, where he expected to find examples of miracles. He earned a Ph.D. at the University of Chicago but, after much study and search, found no help as to how to heal. Then began years of meditation, study, and worldwide searching through Japan, China, and India. In about 15 years, Dr. Usui had learned eight languages and then proceeded to learn Sanskrit. In reading the ancient Sutras he found what he thought was the answer—a formula.

Dr. Usui went to Mt. Kuiyama, Japan, for 21 days of meditation. He took 21 stones to keep track of the number of days gone by. These 21 days were spent in meditation. He had taken only water to sustain him, expecting a phenomena or miracle to occur. Just before the dawn of the 21st day, he saw a candle light at a distance coming toward him. It came closer and closer, getting brighter and brighter. He wondered whether to duck or let it hit him. Then he remembered the reason for being there and decided he should face it. The light hit him between his eyes and knocked him unconscious. He thought he had died. When he awoke the sun was up, and bubbles of light were in front of him with all the colors of the rainbow at first. Then a brilliant white light turned into the formula he had found in the Sutras.

He hurried down the mountain and tore his toe on a stone. He stopped and held his toe with both hands. When the pain stopped and he removed his hands, to his amazement the toe was healed (1st miracle.) Continuing on his way he came upon a man with a table along the road with food (tea, salted plums, and salted cabbage). Being very hungry, Dr. Usui asked for some food. The man said no, that after not eating for 21 days that kind of food would make him sick. Then the man's daughter, who suffered from a skin condition, came out. Dr. Usui asked if he could try to help her. Receiving permission, he placed his hands on her cheeks, and she was healed (2nd miracle). He then insisted on eating the food requested and did so with no problems afterward (3rd miracle). Back at the monastery he healed a monk of arthritis (4th miracle).

Dr. Usui decided the best way to use this gift was to help the needy, the beggars, and he was accepted into the beggars' compound, and given room and board. For seven years he healed them so they could work. Then he started to see those he healed years before revert to their old ways and asked them why. They said they did not like the responsibility. He realized that to be well not only the physical but the spiritual had to be healed. That is when he received the five spiritual aspects of Reiki. These are:

1. Today I will count my many blessings.
2. Just for today I will not worry.
3. Just for today I will not be angry.
4. Today I will do my work honestly.
5. Today I will be kind to every living creature and to my neighbor.

Dr. Usui went back to Kyoto and walked around the compound with a lighted torch. When asked why he did this, he would ask the person to come to his church, and they would hear why. And so he began to teach Reiki. One of the Masters trained by him was Dr. Hiyashi who in turn was the teacher of Mrs. Takata. It was due to Takata that Reiki has been preserved. She was the only Reiki Master left after World War II. She taught in 4 days what it took her 2 years to learn.

Reiki cannot be taught as ordinary knowledge. It must be transmitted like light waves by the meditation and touch of a Reiki Master to a student. Then the method of using the touch is taught through information and demonstration. Reiki heals the cause of illness and eliminates it. One does not have to alter his state of consciousness or go through mental concentration or exercises for Reiki to be effective, nor does the client have to believe Reiki will heal him. Once initiated into the first degree, any student can heal by gently placing hands on the person needing healing.

There is a method of absent healing that is taught in the second degree of Reiki attunement and instruction. Reiki can also be used on plants, animals, and even inanimate objects.

There are two different organizations which have Masters who teach Reiki. They are **THE RADIANCE TECHNIQUE ASSOCIATION INTERNATIONAL** (formerly The American-International Reiki Association) formed by Barbara Ray and the **REIKI ALLIANCE** formed by Takata's granddaughter, Phyllis Furumoto. If you are interested in learning Reiki, contact these organizations for the Master nearest you. The addresses are:

The Radiance Technique Ass. International
P.O. Box 40570
St. Petersburg, FL 33743
(813) 347-3421

Reiki Alliance
P.O. Box 41
Cataldo, ID 83810
(208) 682-3535

Dr. Makao Usui

Hawayo Takata

CHAPTER 6

Polarity Therapy

The human body is wonderfully and marvelously made. There is truly a great Creator behind the design of the form that houses a Divine Spark or Spirit. The Creator, an engineering genius, designed the body with wireless currents of energy continually renewing and powering the form. These are currents which, like electricity, have positive and negative charges. These currents can be brought into balance by the hands and there are grooves or hollow places on the body where a human hand fits perfectly. The Creator designed the body so it can be kept in a healthy state, and when imbalance occurs, there are methods for regaining the energy balance through certain techniques. Polarity Therapy is one of these techniques.

Dr. Randolph Stone, the creator of Polarity Therapy, was born in Austria in 1890. He came to the United States as a boy and became a citizen. He had a thirst for knowledge and became a chiropractor, osteopath, and naturopath and practiced for over 50 years. Dr. Stone searched for more complete forms of healing and studied eastern methods such as acupuncture, herbology, Eastern massage, and the ancient art of healing using the subtle electromagnetic fields of the body as taught by Dr. Paracelsus Von Hohenheim in the 15th century. Polarity Therapy is based on the theory that there is a pattern of energy in the human body that the body uses to heal itself. This is known in the East as Prana (breath) or Chi (Life Force).

In his book **"HEALTH BUILDING"** (page 57), Dr. Stone writes: "The human body is a magnified cell, the expansion of the brain pattern of the airy neuter, all-present Life Energy Principle, which has its base in the cerebrospinal fluid—in the brain and in the spinal cord and throughout the entire nervous system. The middle of the human body is the neuter pole—from the top of the head down through the spinal cord and its three coverings. The cerebrospinal fluid flows between the pia mater and the arachnoid sheets, and follows the nerves all through the body. The right side of the body and the right side of the head is the positive pole. It gives off positive energy currents. The left side of the body and brain is the negative pole, and radiates negative energy currents. This knowledge and awareness can be used by every person to balance his or her own energies and thus relieve pain."

Principles of Polarity

1.   Energy exists in everything and energy makes the form. Example: Iron filings on paper over a magnet display the energy pattern of the magnetic field.

2.   Energy is polarized. Opposites stimulate each other in resistance and balance in exhaustion or in the creation of a new unit.

3.   There is a neuter center of balance. Currents oppose on the surface and unite in the center. A charge moves out of the center, splits into positive and negative charges. There is an outward (centrifugal) movement and an inward (centripetal) movement. This is how life is sustained.

Aspects of Polarity

1.   **Unconditional Love** – Dr. Stone taught that Love is the universal energy that controls all things. In his Forward to Dr. Stone's book, **HEALTH BUILDING**, Dr. Robert K. Hall says of Dr. Stone: "Those of us

who were fortunate enough to have stood with him and received his transmission were imprinted indelibly by his enthusiastic wisdom. Often, in these inspired texts, the very spirit of our old teacher speaks. He looks out at us again from behind a sentence stuffed with meaning, and points to the truth of God's love, found in the human body, the temple more real than all the world's cathedrals."

2. **Mental attitude** – Energy follows thought, so it is important to have positive thoughts. The Life Force flows through the body as if it were following an invisible circulatory system. Mental and emotional blocks also cause physical blocks. We cannot think negative thoughts and have a healthy body. Nothing else in life is as important to a human being as discovering and controlling the life forces through inspiration and higher vision. Thus may the person control their own mind, emotions and senses.

3. **Nutrition** – Disease can be caused by a failure to properly nourish the body. In addition to pure thoughts, pure air, and pure water, we must follow a diet of fresh vegetables, fruits, seeds, nuts, grains, and sprouts. Try to cook the food without killing the enzymes (temperature of less than 110 F.) by using a Chinese wok. Baking and

steaming are good. Avoid frying.

Try to eat 80% alkaline food, and 20% acid food to keep your body in balance. See Appendix on page 112 for a chart showing the alkalinity and acidity of various foods.

4. **Movement** – There is no energy flow without movement because the Life Force becomes stagnant. Exercise is necessary for health. Dr. Stone developed easy stretching postures for releasing the energy flow. Sound also stimulates the central core. The "grunt" arouses latent life forces lying dormant in the body. Breathing activates the solids, liquids, and gases and causes them to be expelled. Breathe deeply, stretch, vibrate with sound, and move to keep the energies flowing.

5. **Polarity Hand Contacts** – There are particular Polarity hand contacts or holds that clear the positive, neuter, and negative poles of the body. This enables the prana, or animating current of life, to flow through the entire system to open up blocked points and establish the proper flow and alignment of Life Force in the body.

Polarity Therapy has been established as a profession. The American Polarity Therapy Association (APTA) has set up standards for certification. An **Associate Polarity Practitioner** is required to complete 155 hours of study and practice in specific areas and a **Registered Polarity Practitioner** is required to have completed at least 615 hours of study and clinical practice. It is not my intention in this book to teach Polarity Therapy. Rather, I wish simply to give illustrations of how to use your hands to balance energies in your body. If you wish to study Polarity Therapy, contact APTA for the teacher nearest you. The address is:

American Polarity Therapy Association
4101 Lake Boone Trail, Suite 201
Raleigh, NC 27607
(919) 787-5181

To help you understand how energy flows in the body, I quote from Dr. Stone: "The human body is a part of space, as a form of Matter, and must be constantly kept in touch with the greater element of space which is Nature as a whole, or it perishes. The energy rhythm of Life must be kept moving through every part of it or it suffers, as well as its four polarized varieties of this element, embodied in four states or kinds of matter, as elements of:

1. Fire, heat, warmth - Energy
2. Air, oxygen - Gas
3. Earth, solids - Food
4. Water, liquids - Beverage

There are four large cavities in the body over which these four polarized energies flow, and organs which act as transformers of these currents, and step down the intensity of the field. These organs also act as converters of energy, extracting from solids, liquids, gases, and heat energy what the body needs for its own fuel and sustenance in order to keep fit as a unit of expression of Mind Energy and Space Substance; but mainly to keep in tune and rhythm with the Universal Field of Nature through the finer and coarser mediums of exchange."

In addition to the four elements of fire, air, earth, and water, there is an ether element which is the link between mind and body. These five elements are represented in the body as follows:

The **Fire Element** represents the Brain and Nervous System.

The **Ether Element** is in the Neck.

The **Air Element** is the Respiratory and Circulatory Systems.

The **Earth Element** is the Digestive System, Assimilation and Elimination.

The **Water Element** represents the Genito-urinary System.

Each part of the body has a positive (+), negative (-) or neuter (0) charge. You can balance energies by knowing the charge of a finger and putting a finger with a different charge opposite it or by putting your hands opposite each other. This creates a flow of energy between the two fingers or hands. A flow of energy thus created, especially if strengthened by mind (visualization) and breath, is stronger than any block to the energy flow in the body. Pain is a block in the energy flow. By releasing the block to the energy flow, dis-ease is eliminated. The word "dis-ease" simply means a distorted energy.

Polarity of Fingers & Toes

The chart below shows the relationship between the polarity of the fingers and toes and the body system each represents.

Digit	Element	Charge	Body System
Thumb & big toe	Ether	0	Joints, head
2nd	Air	-	Respiratory & Circulatory
3rd	Fire	+	Digestive
4th	Water	-	Genito-urinary
5th	Earth	+	Elimination

There are several ways to make contacts on the body; side-to-side, top-to-bottom or front-to-back. The illustrations on page 51 show how to make these contacts on the head. By placing your hands in these positions, you create a current of energy between the positive right hand and the negative left hand. The current of energy thus created can move "stuck" or blocked energy which causes pain and/or congestion. These contacts or hand holds are used to relieve headaches, sinus congestion, earaches, tension or other discomfort in the head. The touch can be light (neuter), strong (positive), or very heavy (negative) depending on the problem. I would suggest starting with a light touch. If the energy block does not move, then increase the pressure.

Differences in the Hands

Right Hand	**Left Hand**
Positive charge	Negative charge
Conducts Sun energy	Conducts Moon energy
Warm	Cool
Gold color	Silver color
Pushes out energy	Receptive, draws in energy

The hands reflect acute conditions in the body and the feet reflect chronic conditions.

Of the hands, Dr. Stone says: "The positive current is the sun energy of fire and radiant warmth in normal amounts. The right

ILLUSTRATIONS

Figure 1.

This is a side-to-side contact.

Figure 2.

This is a top-to-bottom contact.

Figure 3.

This is a front-to-back contact.

hand is the conductor of this energy. For negative tension, congestion, spasm, and stasis, the right hand contains the antidote, the positive polarity current. The left hand is the conductor of the negative or moon current, which is cooling, soothing, refreshing, and toning. Place it over the seat of pain, where the positive currents are in excess, giving the symptoms mentioned above. Wherever the pain is, that excess calls for the release of the irritation, heat, and swelling, which the negative current can provide."

The human body is a microcosm to the macrocosm of the universe, and each cell in the body is a microcosm to the macrocosm of the body. Within the body are many patterns or fields of energy. Dr. Stone describes how the body continually tries to balance itself.

From *Book III: Polarity Therapy* by Dr. Stone: "The gross body is made of two pattern fields or halves. The right half of the body is a positive pattern field in total, made up of subsidiary fields. The left half of the body is a negative pattern field, having subsidiary polarity fields in its make-up. The upper portion of the body, above the diaphragm, is the positive field equivalent unto the heavens which give air, warmth, and energy for the sustenance of life. The diaphragm is the firmament which separates the above from the below and is its neuter field; the portion below the diaphragm is the neuter pole equivalent to the earth which nourishes all creatures, just as the neuter pole in the body nourishes all cells. The pelvis is the negative pole.

The vital life-breath current flows through all three fields and polarizes them into active functions. The current crosses over in each field or oval of matter space in the body, producing a neuter center of function in each field. By linking these five ovals in a connected line or current and crossing them over at each center, the mysterious serpentine force of the Caduceus is brought to light. This is the oldest symbol of the chain effect of the vital body in the gross physical one, and it is the sign and symbol of the physician from ancient times up to the present.

....Life proceeds from within outward and from above downward.

....In dis-ease the finer currents are not flowing through the denser fields of the body, or they are blocked and act excessively at the points of resistance, which appear as symptoms and intense, acute pains. This clearly indicates that the best therapy is that which balances the forces in that particular individual with his inner center of gravity, around which these currents revolve. In this manner the normal attractive power of the current is re-established with the Whole. The outside cosmic field is the reservoir where this supply comes from for the function of the denser particles of matter, which keeps the body as a unit representative here among all the five aspects of matter in their three modes of motion.

....The five separate currents which make a complete circuit on each half of the body, flowing near the surface, from the head to the five fingers and to the five toes, are sensory currents. These flow in a straight line and can be treated with good results, especially at their terminating poles, as powerful sensory reactions for relief of stagnant sensory energy blocks. These five sensory currents themselves do not cross over, so as not to mix sensory impressions. But, for the best results in therapy, they are used as bipolar contacts, either from top to bottom, or reverse, or from side to side, depending on the direction of flow of the currents treated.

....Also, excellent results can be obtained by a contact with the finger and thumb of one hand on the toe of one foot of the client, and with the other contact on the corresponding joint and toe of the client's other foot.

...The same can be done with the fingers on each hand of the client, for polarizing the neuter pole in the extremities.

...This polarizes the current of one side with the other side and elicits quick and favorable responses from the corresponding reflexes."

The placement of your hands for balancing the longitudinal currents are shown in the following illustrations. Figure 4 shows

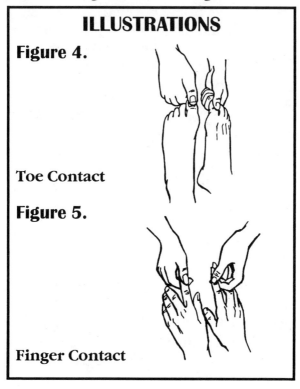

ILLUSTRATIONS

Figure 4.

Toe Contact

Figure 5.

Finger Contact

the hand contacts for the toes and Figure 5 the hand contacts for the fingers.

Hand Contacts

Dr. Stone explained how the hand contacts work in bringing in the flow of energy to the body. In addition to placing the hands on the head, toes and fingers, you can place your hands on the whole body to balance the positive, neuter and negative poles. Since energy flows from above downward, start with one hand (called north pole hand) on the positive pole or head of the client and the other hand (called south pole hand) on the diaphragm or neuter pole of the body. (See Figure 6.) Hold until you can feel the energy flowing between your hands. When the energy is flowing well (feels tingly), move your north pole or upper hand to the diaphragm and your south pole or lower hand to the pelvic area. (See Figure 7.) Again, hold until you feel the energy flowing.

There are positive, neuter, and negative zones for each of the elements. If there is a specific problem area of the body, determine which element or body system is involved. Then clear the three poles or triads of that element. **EXAMPLE:** For headache or digestive problems, the fire element needs to be balanced. To do this, put one hand on the

56

ILLUSTRATIONS

Figure 6

Figure 7

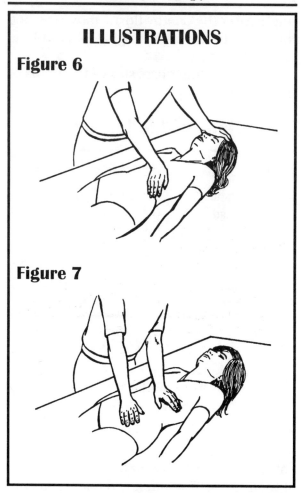

head and the other hand on the solar plexus.
When the energy flows between your hands,
move them down so the top hand is on the
solar plexus and the bottom hand is on one

thigh. After the energy flows, move the bottom hand to the other thigh. Hold until the energy flows.

The following chart shows the triads of the elements.

Triads of the Elements

Element	Positive Pole	Neuter Pole	Negative Pole
Air	Shoulders	Kidneys	Ankles
Fire	Head	Gall bladder	Thighs
Water	Breasts (Hold on back of body)	Genitals	Feet
Earth	Neck	Colon	Knees

General Balancing

You can give an all over, general balancing to someone by holding the following six positions. Hold each position lightly until the energy flows.

Position # 1 - Sit at the head of the client and gently place your hands on the sides of their head. The index and middle fingers go down the sides of the neck; the thumb rests by the ear.

Position # 2 - Get on the right side of the client. Gently rest your left hand on their forehead and your right hand on the bottom of the rib cage.

Position # 3 - Stay on the right side and place your right hand on the client's left hip bone while your left hand goes on their right shoulder.

Position # 4 - Go to the client's left side. Place your left hand on their right hip and your right hand on their left shoulder.

Position # 5 - Stay on the left side. Hold the client's right foot (at the arch) with your left hand and their left hand with your right hand.

Position # 6 - Go to the right side. Hold the client's left foot with your right hand and their right hand with your left hand.

You have now balanced all the elements in the body. The client should feel very relaxed but energized. This is the basis of Polarity Therapy.

Polarity Circle

If you are working with a group of people, have six people work on one person. Put the receiver on a treatment table and assign each of the six positions defined above. This will create a circuit of loving energy for the seventh person (receiver).

One person should direct the procedure. Have the givers rub their hands together vigorously for half a minute, then place their hands on the receiver and close their eyes. Persons holding positions three and four (shoulders and hips) should work together and gently rock the hips. (Do not rock the shoulders.) All should begin to tone the "OM." Send love, "OM," and rock from five to ten minutes. The leader uses intuition to determine the length of time. Then gently bring the rocking and "OMing" to a halt but keep the hands in place while continuing to send love. The energy flow will slow down, then stop. At that point have all slowly lift their hands off the person but hold them several inches above the position. When sensation stops, take the hands away, shake them, then rinse in cold water. This grounds and removes the static energy. Have the receiver sit up slowly and drink a glass of water, juice, or herbal tea.

This is an excellent technique to use with children. They enjoy doing the polarity circle and even very young children can learn this easily.

Dr. Stone also taught head molding therapy and its effects on body areas. He talked of energy fields or life energy currents of prana that flow through the central core and nerve centers. He said, "The moulding process involved directional force used plus the polarity reflexes. The central axis of the body's energy field is definitely influenced by external impulses of energy applied which reacts through the wireless energy whirls, flowing through the meninges like an induced current and affects the tension of the cerebrospinal fluids locally. The skull is a hollow band shell in which the ultrasonic energy current of the soul reverberates like the music of the spheres and is thus broadcasted; the brain acting as the converter and switchboard for the whole body." Dr. Stone asked, "Is it possible that these five bones of the sacrum have a definite relationship to the five bones on the top of the head like the foundation of a house has to its roof? These five bones are moulds or tattwas and the five life energy currents of prana flowing through their central contents and nerve centers." (Chart 43 of **"THE WIRELESS ANATOMY OF MAN"**.) Whole treatment sessions were taught using these principles.

American Polarity Therapy Association

Anyone interested in finding a Polarity

Practitioner in their area or in studying Polarity Therapy can obtain information from:

American Polarity Therapy Association
4101 Lake Boone Trail
Suite 201
Raleigh, NC 27607-6518
(919) 787-5181

Randolph Stone, D.O.

CHAPTER 7

Zero Balancing

Fritz Smith, M.D. has developed a body handling system, known as Zero Balancing (ZB), which focuses on the interface between body energy and body structure. It is a form of structural acupressure in which the hands are used to create a fulcrum, or still point, around which energy and structure can balance, and dysfunction can normalize.

Zero Balancing focuses to a great extent on the skeletal system of the body because the deepest, strongest currents of energy are conducted by bone, the densest tissue in the body. One of the principles of ZB is that, if we put a clearer, stronger force field through a body part, the currents and vibrations in that part will release any "held tension patterns" and become more organized and balanced. By putting in these vectors of force, we remove or reorganize blocked energy and bring harmony and balance to the energy and structure of the body. We ease dis-ease. Many of these held energy patterns are beneath the level of our conscious awareness. The integration often occurs on a sub-liminal level and eases emotional trauma without the reliving or re-experience of the trauma. This is particularily valuable on the level of the cellular memory of the body and in cases where physical injury occurred at the time of high emotional stress.

In an interview for **"INTERFACE,"** the newsletter for zero balancers, Dr. Smith states: "Through ZB we now know we can directly influence tissue memory and cellular content but ZB has another characteristic which makes it a special skill in the therapeutic world. Through ZB, the direct experience of the moment can be incorporated into a fulcrum and used as a working tool.... It is through direct experience that we know the world, regardless of whether the experience comes through touch, sight, smell, hearing, proprioception and so on. If a fulcrum engenders an experience which is contrary to, or different from previous ones, and if the new experience is intense enough or repeated often enough, it can help to reprogram the body/mind. These fulcrums can give a person a different orientation to the world, with options that promote a response

For the skilled body worker, new concepts and understandings concerning the structural/energetic interface usually emerge which enhance the person's existing skills. For the acupuncturist, understanding the body side of the body/energy equation provides a means of opening structural blocks which can impede the acupuncture treatments.

"The Core Zero Balancing program is taught in two 30-hour workshops (ZB Core I & ZB Core II) separated by 6 or more months. The ZB Core I program reviews basic concepts from Western science (particularly anatomy, physiology, and kinesiology) and basic concepts of Eastern teaching (including energy, chakras, and mechanisms of healing). With this information as background, the foundations of Zero Balancing are presented, with emphasis of hands-on understanding and experience. At the end of this five day program, the participant can actually use the Zero Balancing system.

"The ZB Core II program repeats the basic five day workshop after a period where Zero Balancing has been practiced. With this practical experience, the intermediate student now hears the presentation from an entirely different perspective, and understandings deepen. The intention of this program is for the person to begin to make the work his or her own. This internal conceptualization represents a fundamental shift in understanding and probably makes this the most important training session.

"The Advanced Classes are designed to answer the needs of the practitioner. These classes may include problem solving, refining touch, or general course correction; they may emphasize new material or advanced understandings of body handling. One underlying theme in all of them is to build a strong support system, a community of practitioners with a common bond and understanding.

"The Master Classes have more to do with looking at the theoretical aspects of structural/energetic healing and in working with one's own personal process in transcending the older models of healing. These workshops are for Certified Zero Balancers and people deeply involved in the program."

"INNER BRIDGES: A GUIDE TO ENERGY MOVEMENT AND BODY STRUCTURE" by Fritz Frederick Smith, M.D. (Humanics Ltd., 1990) is a book which is recommended reading for general information and as background for any of the classes.

To obtain information on finding a Zero

Balancing practitioner near you or about classes, write or call:

The Zero Balancing Association
P.O. Box 1727
Capitola, CA 95010
(408) 476-0665

Fritz Smith, M.D.

CHAPTER 8

Craniosacral Therapy

The osteopathic profession has worked with cranial motion and its effect on body systems since the early 1900s. Some outstanding practitioners who helped develop craniosacral therapy are Dr. William Sutherland and John E. Upledger, D.O.

William Sutherland studied at the American School of Osteopathy in Kirkville, Missouri in the early 1900s. He was fascinated with the design of the bones of the human skull. By experimenting on himself and others, Sutherland was able to feel minute cranial motions and found that the sacrum moved in synchrony with the cranium. He developed a model showing that the rhythmic contraction and expansion of the ventricle system of the brain moves the cerebrospinal fluid which moves the sphenoid which drives the rest of the cranial movement. His work has been the basis for teaching osteopaths.

Dr. Upledger was a professor in the Department of Biomechanics, College of Osteopathic Medicine at Michigan State University and chief of staff at the Unity Center for Health, Education, and Research in Palm Beach, Florida. He has developed a model for teaching craniosacral therapy that shows the craniosacral system as a semi-closed hydraulic system formed by the dura mater membrane and its contents. Dr. Upledger and Jon D. Vredevoogd, M.F.A. have co-authored a book titled **"CRANIOSACRAL THERAPY"** which is published by Eastland Press in Seattle. This book defines the physiology and anatomy of the craniosacral system and presents practical methods of using this knowledge to treat diseases that affect various organ systems. Simply using your hands as preceptors, and the intention of assisting the body to self-correct, can bring about therapeutic results.

In Craniosacral work, the body fascia is involved. The fascia is a continuous laminated sheath of connective tissue which surrounds all of the somatic and visceral structures of the human body. The loss of mobility of the fascia can be used to find the location of a disease process. The whole body moves (imperceptible to the eyes but can be felt with the hands) when the cerebrospinal fluid pumps between the brain and the end of the spine (sacrum). This cyclical flexion and extension occurs at a rate of approximately 6 to 12 cycles per minute. Restrictions of the movement in the bands of fascia are released so the body can self heal.

A technique called using direction of energy or "V-spread" is also used to release restrictions. A "V-spread" consists of putting two fingers of one hand on either side of a restriction and holding fingers of the other hand opposite the restriction place on the body. Just as in the chapter on Polarity Therapy you learned that the fingers have negative and positive charges, in Craniosacral Therapy you use your fingers as electrodes and visualize a current passing between them. You are sending an electrical energy between your hands and through the client's body. This current moves the energy block and allows the body to heal.

Many conditions are helped by Craniosacral Therapy. It helps the body to rebalance and heal. It also releases emotions (called somatoemotional recall and release or "unwinding"). A session removes stress from the cellular memory.

If you wish to experience or study Craniosacral Therapy, contact the Upledger Institute for the address of a practitioner or classes near you. The address is:

Upledger Institute
11211 Prosperity Farms Road
Palm Beach Gardens, FL 33410
1-800-233-5880

John E. Upledger, D.O.

CHAPTER 9

Acupressure

Acupressure has been used in the Orient for thousands of years, but only within the last twenty years or so has it been recognized in western countries as a therapeutic method. The Chinese pressure points of pain have been illustrated very specifically for various problems. The Chinese doctors insert needles into the meridians and control points. Since I have not studied acupuncture, I will not discuss it and will limit this chapter to the use of fingers on the control points.

There are diagrams of the body showing where to place your fingers for the relief of pain and to stimulate energy movement.

Some books that illustrate these diagrams are: "ACUPUNCTURE WITHOUT NEEDLES" and "HANDBOOK OF UNUSUAL AND UNORTHODOX HEALING METHODS" both by J.V. Cerney, D.C., A.B., D.M., D.P.M., and published by Parker Publishing Company, and **"HIGH TECH TOUCH: ACUPRESSURE IN THE SCHOOLS"** written by Jeanne St. John and published by Academic Therapy Publications.

I have used pressure points illustrated in Cerney's books and found them very effective. Those which relate to the back of the body are very similar to the points used for Zero Balancing fulcrums. Points on the back are related to all the internal organs and the head. There are diagrams showing the acupressure points to use for problems from arthritis, asthma, colitis, gastritis, heart, incontinence, migraines, sciatica, sex organs, stress, whiplash, and everything in between. Using these points to move energy through the body is a way to keep yourself healthy.

As the mother of five children and grandmother to eight, I am always looking for ways to enhance the physical, emotional, and mental health of children. When I read **"HIGH TECH TOUCH: ACUPRESSURE IN THE SCHOOLS"** by Jeanne St. John, I was impressed to get information about the book to as many teachers as possible, especially those who teach special education. Jeanne St. John had been a patient of Dr. Fritz Smith (see chapter on Zero Balancing) and had been relieved of migraines by his application of acupuncture.

Ms. St. John was appointed as principal in special education and had to deal with children with physical, emotional, and mental problems. When her school nurse suggested that acupressure might be helpful to the students, a six-week project was developed to test the idea. The results of the project (improvement in physical mobility, classroom behavior, and academic performance) were so significant that other teachers were trained and the use of acupressure expanded in Santa Cruz County school system.

The **PRESS** (Physical Response Education System) Project at the Santa Cruz County Office of Education has given workshops at hundreds of state, national, and international conferences teaching the acupressure points used in the project. These acupressure techniques have been used on teachers, parents, and senior citizens to great advantage. One of the most significant uses has been to promote optimal change and development in normal or handicapped children.

Project PRES has developed audio-visual aids, workbooks, and charts for use in elementary and secondary schools. Some of the information available is:

High Tech: Acupressure in the Schools - Manual (# 567-7)

Elementary Classroom Packet (# 568-5)
Secondary Classroom Packet (# 569-3)
Audio Tape Cassette by Jeanne St. John
(# 570-7) (this is 60 minutes and contains Energy Exercises, 30 point locations and neck releases)

Write for ordering information and prices to:

Academic Therapy Publications
20 Commercial Boulevard
Novato, CA 94947-6191

I suggest that all who are concerned with the optimum growth of their children should obtain information about acupressure and get this information to the teachers of their school system. Parents can use these techniques on their children to make positive changes in their attitude, behavior, academic and athletic performance, and on each other to relieve the stresses of daily living. The head, neck, and shoulder points illustrated at the end of the chapter are taken from a relatively new system of Jin Shin Do® developed by Iona Marsaa Teeguarden, M.A. Her book, **"ACUPRESSURE WAY OF HEALTH: JIN SHIN DO"** was published in 1978 and includes information on energy flow, point location, and how to give a traditional acupressure session. Some of her other books are: **"THE JOY OF FEELING: BODYMIND**

ACUPRESSURE" which describes the relationship between energy flow and emotional responses; **"FUNDAMENTALS OF SELF-ACUPRESSURE"** which is particularly useful to the beginner; and **"A COMPLETE GUIDE TO ACUPRESSURE"** edited by Iona Marsaa Teeguarden, Japan Publications, 1993. To order these books, or for information on Jin Shin Do® Bodymind Acupressure™ contact:

The Jin Shin Do® Foundation for Bodymind Acupressure™
366 CAlifornia Avenue, Suite 16
Palo Alto, CA 94306
(415) 328-1811
or
P.O. Box 1097
Felton, CA 95018

Another source of acupressure information is available from Aminah Raheem, Ph.D. Her books **"SOUL RETURN: INTEGRATING BODY, PSYCHE AND SPIRIT"** and **"PROCESS ACUPRESSURE"** can be ordered from:

Aminah Raheem, Ph.D.
P.O. Box 1727,
Capitola, CA 95010.
Phone (408) 476-0665.

Aminah Raheem, Ph.D.

Basic Neck and Shoulder Release*

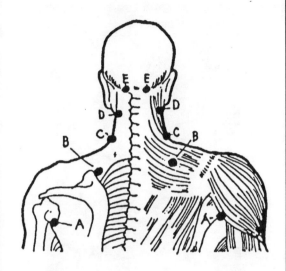

1. The neck release is the last pattern (before finishing points) in a traditional acupressure session. Most of the energy meridians flow through this area, creating a "bottleneck" of energy blockage in many people.

2. In traditional acupressure sessions, the receiver lies on a table, but the method also works well when receiver is sitting. Receiver guides giver to the most sensitive spot in area.

3. With the receiver either sitting or lying comfortably, face-up in a relaxed position, the giver applies fingertip pressure at the point indicated in the diagram (left hand on left side, right hand on right side). The giver and receiver breathe deeply throughout.

4. Giver uses comfortably firm fingertip pressure, holding each set of pressure points for one to two minutes, or until the muscle relaxes. With practice, one learns to feel the pulse at the points and eventually "balance" them into synchronous pulsations.

5. If receiver is light-headed or dizzy after a neck release, hold ankles or do leg lift and pull.

Point A—Place fingertips under the outside of the shoulders at Points A. Curl fingertips and press gently but firmly.

Point B—Press thumbs in hollows at top of inside shoulder blades, at Point B.

Point C—Press trapezius muscle at base of neck, top of shoulder, Point C. Use thumbs or fingers gently as this point is often very tender.

Point D—Using thumb and middle finger, press mid-way up neck, outside spine, and behind ears, at Point D. Hold forehead with L hand.

Point E—With thumb and middle finger, hold Point E, the hollows at the base of the skull. Hold forehead with L hand.

* Adapted from **"THE ACUPRESSURE WAY OF HEALTH: JIN SHIN DO"** by Iona Marsaa Teeguarden, Japan Publications, 1978, pp. 120-123.

CHAPTER 10

Color Healing

Light, through the interplay with darkness, creates color. Ancient Wisdom teaches that the Supreme Creator originally filled space at the beginning of manifestation with His Aura, permeating every atom of the cosmos with life force. We have now reached materiality and the outcome of the future is an upward advancement into the higher vibration. The color rays are pouring down on earth night and day.

Human beings are very sensitive to color. Our skins are light sensitive, thus color sensitive. The nerve endings issue a fine chemical that is individually adjusted to each of us and filters light. We are all different and absorb according to our own sensitivity. The nerve ends take the color back to the pituitary gland which causes the entire body to react. **EXAMPLE:** When red light is shown on a body, the cells compact (have no gaps) and therefore red light raises blood pressure. Blue light makes the cells hold together more loosely, so it lowers the blood pressure.

Light reacts faster than pigment. The science of color is based on the fact that matter and light are fundamentally inseparable and that when solid matter is reduced to its essence, it becomes converted into a radiation identical with light. Color is a vibration of matter, and our souls reflect it into the three-dimensional world through atomic patterns. These patterns, or our "aura," are there for those who can see them. Clairvoyants are able to see the colors in our aura and determine the state of our health.

There are seven colors which come from the Sun and ray out from the nucleus of a tiny atom. We see this light as the colors of the rainbow. These seven colors correspond to the seven major glands, or energy centers in our bodies, called "chakras" in eastern wisdom. Color is the bridge between the seen and unseen worlds. We pass over this bridge into new and different states of consciousness when we use color, which is a manifestation of Divine Mind. Color is as necessary to the soul as air is to the body. The soul rejoices and lives in color.

Color, when used in the right shades and focused onto the right place, can correct disharmonies in our aura and restore the body to health. Color healing can be done through visualizing the color, using music which correlates to color, using colored lights on the body and drinking water which has been put in the sun in colored bottles.

Color therapy was used thousands of years ago by the Chinese. They built gazebos with beautiful silk screens in the colors of the rainbow. People would sit in these gazebos on a sunny day. The sun shining through the colored silk would put the color of that screen onto their body and thus transfer that energy into them. The Egyptians, Greeks and Romans used the same idea getting the value of color into the body by having the sun shine through colored silk or glass. Hippocrates, Paracelsus, Da Vinci, and Goethe used color. In fact, it is believed by many people that the whole reason for the development of stained glass windows was a spiritual form of color therapy.

Each of the seven colors relate to a certain endocrine gland, chakra, gem, metal, planet, astrological sign, musical note, and has characteristic qualities.

The chart on the following pages illustrates these correspondences.

COLOR	RED	ORANGE	YELLOW	GREEN
GLAND	Sacral plexus	Spleen	Pancreas, adrenals	Thymus
CHAKRA	Root	Splenic	Solar Plexus	Heart
GEM	Ruby	Amber	Topaz	Emerald
METAL	Iron	Gold	Copper	Silver
PLANET	Mars	Sun	Mercury	Saturn
SIGN	Aries Scorpio	Leo	Taurus Libra	Cancer
NOTE	C	D	E	F
QUALITY	Life, strength, vitality, power	Courage, self-confidence, optimism	Joy, mental power, happiness	Hope, love, healing, balance

COLOR	BLUE	INDIGO	VIOLET
GLAND	Thyroid	Pineal	Pituitary
CHAKRA	Throat	Third Eye	Crown
GEM	Sapphire	Jet	Amethyst
METAL	Lead	Chromium	Tin
PLANET	Venus	Uranus	Jupiter
SIGN	Capricorn Sagittarius	Aquarius, Pisces	Gemini, Virgo
NOTE	G	A	B
QUALITY	Inspiration, creativity, faith, devotion	Intuition, spiritual perception	Humility, creative imagination, divine realization

People's systems are different and will react to color on a very individual basis. However, most systems of color therapy agree on the use of certain colors for specific problems. These are given here.

Red

It vitalizes and stimulates so it is good for anemia, colds, blood deficiency, circulatory problems, low blood pressure, arthritis, paralysis, and tiredness. It is cheerful and warming and helps heal bones. An excess of red can cause one to be hyperactive. Blue is its complementary color.

Orange

Stimulates the spleen, is warm and positive. It helps in the regulation of food intake and in the assimilation and circulation processes. Cures paralysis due to emotional reaction. Orange induces tolerance and strengthens the will. It relieves repression and stimulates mental activity and combines physical energy with mental wisdom. It helps allergies, asthma, kidney problems, gall stones, bronchitis, epilepsy, general nervous debility and mental problems. Orange is used in treating the lungs, thyroid, cramps, and in strengthening bones, teeth, and in curing rickets. It is associated with the mineral calcium. An excess of orange may lead to an indulgent behavior where a balance leads to a sense of freedom from limitation. Violet is its complementary color.

Yellow

This color has a positive effect on the nerves, the mind, and the soul, and inspires and illuminates a person mentally. It is good for stomach and liver problems, diabetes, diarrhea, constipation, eczema, skin diseases, nervous exhaustion, and indigestion. It helps rheumatism, genital problems, jaundice, and relieves mental depression. An excess of yellow can cause one to be stimulated mentally too much and be prone to nervous exhaustion and neglect of the physical body. A lack of yellow causes diabetes, digestive troubles, and overweight. Violet is its complementary color.

Green

Green stimulates the heart center, brings balance, and is calming to the nerves. It soothes the nervous system and cools the blood. As it is the balance between the red and blues, it is the master healer. It stimulates the master gland, the pituitary, dissolves clots and congestions, eliminates toxins and germs, regulates the liver, and builds tissue of skin and muscle. Lack of green causes heart trouble, high blood pressure, neuralgia, ulcers, cancer, syphilis, fidgeting, exhaustion, fatigue, and depression. An excess of green would lead one to love abnormally, to be unbalanced in that one would attempt to do too many things at once and therefore be fatigued. Magenta is its complementary color.

Blue

Blue is antidote to red. If red increases blood pressure, blue decreases it; where red increases plant growth, blue retards it; where red increases hormonal activity, blue decreases it. Blue helps to dissolve fat, works with the glands and fat system of the body, helps throat problems and insomnia. It is an antiseptic so it relieves gum and tooth pain, fevers, shock, headaches, vomiting, inflamed bowels, cuts, stings, burns, itches, and childhood diseases.

Blue is a spiritual color and brings love, peace, healing, serenity, inspiration, and unselfishness. An excess of blue can bring depression. Its complementary color is red.

Indigo

This is the color of intuition. New ideas and inventions will come to those on this ray. It is concerned with mental and psychic facilities and dispels negativity. Indigo stimulates body, mind, and spirit. It brings tranquility, a sense of at-one-ment, and purifies the blood. It can be used to treat problems of the eyes, ears, nose, facial paralysis, asthma, bronchitis, pneumonia and lung diseases. It helps to relieve swelling and pain. An excess of indigo would be associated with mental confusion and a lack of control of one's mental faculties. A balance of indigo would bring clear perception, logical thought, and increased enlightenment. Its complementary color is orange.

Violet

Violet is the color of power and accomplishment. It stimulates the spiritual path, brings self esteem, poise, inspiration, peace, love, and great achievement. Do not use violet on undeveloped minds. Use violet for nervous disorders, with scalp and skin problems, bladder and overactive kidneys, epilepsy, concussion, overactive glands, headaches, tumors, baldness, rheumatism. For cancer, first send violet, then use green. It stimulates the spleen and builds white blood cells. Yellow is its complementary color.

Color in Food

It is important that we feed our bodies food of all the colors. Each day we should also have food of each element. Some of the foods of each element are shown in the chart below:

	AIR	**FIRE**	**WATER**	**EARTH**
Quality-	Sour	Bitter	Salty	Sweet
	nuts	grains	celery	fats
	citrus	seeds	melons	starches
	tomatoes	lentils	cucumbers	sugars
	strawberries	legumes	pumpkin	tubers
	rhubarb	soybeans	leafy veggies	
	strong cheeses	berries	watery fruits	
	yogurt			
	sour milk			
	buttermilk			
Grow-	High in air	Within reach	On ground	In ground

Air foods are from flowers and are usually yellow. Fire foods are red. Water foods are mostly green. Earth foods are brown or orange.

Red, orange, and yellow foods have an alkaline effect. Green foods are neither acid or alkaline, they are neutral. Blue, indigo, and violet foods have an acid effect.

As you can see from the above chart, food is complex and is not strictly one element or color. **EXAMPLE:** A red apple contains all elements since the red skin is fire, the white flesh is water, the seed pod is air, and the sweetness is earth. Carrots are earth but since they have an orange color, they also have some fire in them. A purple potato will have some fire energy while the white potato will not. Broccoli is a flower and therefore an air food but, since it is green, it has water in it also. If we are careful to use food from each of the elements and some of each color, we will have a truly balanced diet.

How to Use Color to Heal

Use gem stones – you can wear a stone of a specific color; or make a distillation of colored water by putting a gemstone in distilled water in the sun for a few days then drink the water; or make a circle of gemstones either actually or by imagination and put yourself into that circle; place a gemstone on an area of the body needing that color; or communicate with the mineral kingdom in meditation and ask their help.

Use color in your environment – Wear clothing of the color you need; paint the walls of your home or office; use bed sheets of the needed color. **NOTE:** Put blue in the bedroom of a hyper child or one with allergies. Put yellow in the room of a shy person or one who needs intellectual stimulation.

Color breathing – Visualize each color separately, breathe in the color and feel it filling your body. Remember that the first three colors (red, orange, yellow) are magnetic and should be visualized as flowing up from the earth towards the solar plexus. The last three (blue, indigo, violet) are electrical and are breathed in from the ether downwards. The green ray is the balancer of the spectrum and flows into the system horizontally.

A variation of color breathing is to visualize each chakra and breathe into that chakra its own color.

Solarized water – This can be done in two ways. Either use a glass bottle of the color you need or take a clear glass bottle and wrap it in theatrical gel of the color. Then put the bottle in the sun for a few days. Drink the water. **NOTE:** If you juice fresh fruits or vegetables and do not drink all the juice immediately, you can put the juice in the sun and the flavor will come back.

Color rubs – Buy cheesecloth or felt and make a 3 1/2 x 4 inch pillow and dye it the color you want. Fill it with 2 cups of raw bran and 1 cup of sea salt. Put it in the sun for several hours. Then rub it on the body where that color is needed. It will last 2 days, then put it back in the sun.

Solar bath – Put theatrical gels on a window and let the sun shine through it and bathe the bare body.

Colored lights – You can obtain colored slides (gels placed between two glass slides) and put them into a slide projector. Put the person needing healing on a chair and shine the light of the projector on them for five minutes. A variation is to use a flood light with a colored gel placed over the light. **NOTE:** There is a Light Center in North Carolina which has a room in which color therapy is used. There are bands of flood lights with colored gel over them placed around a circular room. There are 11 chairs to seat people. Music plays during the color session. Each color of the rainbow is separately shone for five minutes with a half minute of darkness between. By meditating or praying while the colors are being shone, a person increases the value of the color session. It brings a balance to the body. The Light Center can be contacted at:

United Research
P.O. Box 1146
Black Mountain, NC 28711
(704) 669-6845

To improve your mood – Color can affect your mood. By understanding how color affects you, this information can be used to make yourself feel better. By surrounding yourself with colors that have a good effect on you, or wearing an uplifting color, you can feel more cheerful and energetic.

Red – stimulates and cheers you up. If you are depressed or feeling lazy, wear red.

Pink – It also stimulates but in a gentler manner than red. Pink has always been associated with good health. Wearing this color not only peps you up but makes you look glowingly healthy. Pink is also the color of love, and being in love naturally keeps one young, so wear pink and look younger.

Orange – This increases enthusiasm and makes you feel better physically. It generates a feeling of well-being, so if your confidence or enthusiasm are down, wear orange.

Yellow – This is the color of intellectual ability. The color stimulates the intellect and is cheerful. If you need to teach or lecture, wear yellow. Put yellow in a study.

Green – This is good for the nerves and is the color of healing. It is soothing and should be used in a room where you want to relax, such as a bedroom or living room.

It is excellent for hospital rooms.

Turquoise – This tranquilizes and decreases activity. If you are nervous or tense, turquoise will help calm you down. It is also a cooling color, so wear it on a hot day, and you won't feel the heat as much.

Blue – This is the ultimate soothing color. It calms you down, aids sleep, and makes you feel secure and comfortable. If you are a poor sleeper, try visualizing blue all around you, and it will help you relax and fall asleep.

Violet – This is a spiritual color of the highest vibration. It will enhance meditation. It benefits the hair, eyes, and digestion. It soothes irritation and excitability and restores dignity and self-respect. DO NOT use violet on undeveloped minds.

Need for a Full-Color Spectrum

Our bodies need sunlight, which contains all the colors of the rainbow. Most of us spend a lot of time under florescent lights, which are not good for our health. However, there are "Full-Spectrum" florescent tubes now available which contain all of the visible light rays. These bulbs are more expensive than the regular bulbs but are healthy to work under because they bring balance to the body.

Weight Loss with Color

The following information was taken from a book titled **"COLOR THERAPY"** by R.B. Amber, published in Calcutta, India, in 1964:

"The body of an overweight person suffers from an insufficiency of red rays because it has an overabundance of blue rays. The body is overdosed with blue rays and underdosed with red rays. Thus, one is encouraged to add red rays by four means: (1) bathe in red light; (2) eat foods embodying the red, or orange or yellow ray; (3) drink red-solarized water; and (4) visualize red and breathe it in through meditation. On the other hand, if one wants to add weight, one should use the same four steps substituting blue light."

CHAPTER 11

References to Other Healing Methods

I have told you about the healing methods that I have used over the years, and given you the addresses and phone numbers to contact those organizations. However, there are many other techniques available, so I have listed places of reference for some of them.

Bodywork

American Massage Therapy Association (AMTA)
1130 W. North Shore Avenue
Chicago, IL 60626-1670
(312) 761-2682

Jin Shin Do© Foundation for Bodymind Acupressure™
P.O. Box 1800
Idyllwild, CA 92349

Self-Therap/Ease
P.O. Box 8014
Calabasas, CA 91302

The Acupressure Institute
1533 Shattuck
Berkeley, CA 94709

Jin Shin Jyutsu
2919 N. 67th Place
Scottsdale, AZ 85251

Touch for Health
1174 North Lake Avenue
Pasadena, CA 91104
(818) 794-1181

International Ass. of Holistic Health Practitioners
3419 Thom Blvd.
Las Vegas, NV 89130
(702) 873-4542

International Institute for Bioenergetic Analysis
144 E. 36th Street
New York, NY 10016
(212) 532-7742

American Holistic Medical Association
4101 Lake Boone Trail, Suite 201
Raleigh, NC 27607
(919) 787-5146

American Oriental Bodywork Therapy Association
50 Maple Place
Manhasset, NY 11030
(516) 365-5025

American Polarity Therapy Association
4101 Lake Boone Trail
Suite 201
Raleigh, NC 27607
(919) 787-5181

American Foundation for Alternative Health Care, Research & Development
25 Landfield Avenue
Monticello, NY 12701
(914) 794-8181
* Serves as an alternative health care resource center. Compiles data and statistics.

American Foundation of Traditional Chinese Medicine
1280 Columbus Avenue, Suite 302
San Francisco, CA 94133
(415) 776-0502

American Healing Association
c/o Rev. Brian Zink
811 Ridge Drive
Glendale, CA 91206

* Psychic, spiritual, faith healing, and counselors.

Feldenkrais Guild
> 524 Ellsworth Street
> P.O. Box 489
> Albany, OR 97321-0143
> (503) 926-0981

Foot Reflexology Awareness Association
> P.O. Box 7622
> Mission Hills, CA 91346-7622
> (818) 361-0528

Hellerwork, Inc.
> 406 Berry Street
> Mt. Shasta, Ca 96067
> 800-392-3900

International College of Applied Kinesiology
> P.O. Box 905
> Lawrence, KS 66044
> (913) 542-1801

International Rolf Institute
> 302 Pearl Street
> Boulder, CO 80306
> (303) 449-5903

North American Society of Teachers of the Alexander Technique
> P.O. Box 3992
> Champaign, IL 61826-3992
> (217) 359-3529

Trager Institute
    33 Millwood
    Mill Valley, CA 94941-2091
    (415) 388-2688

Alliance/Foundation for Alternative Medicine
    160 NW Widmer Place
    Albany, OR 97321
    (503) 926-4678

Other Therapies

National Federation of Spiritual Healers of America, Inc.
    P.O. Box 2022
    Mt. Pleasant, SC 29465
    (803) 849-1529
    * Spiritual healing

Center for Attitudinal Healing
    19 Main Street
    Tiburon, CA 94920
    (415) 435-5022

International Ass. for Neuro-Linguistic Programming
    310 N. Alabama, Suite A100
    Indianapolis, IN 46204
    (317) 636-6059

National Association for Music Therapy
    8455 Colesville Road, Suite 930
    Silver Spring, MD 20910
    (301) 589-3300

American Art Therapy Association
1202 Allanson Road
Mundelein, IL 60060
(708) 949-6064

American Dance Therapy Association
2000 Century Plaza, Suite 108
Columbia, MD 21044
(410) 997-4040

Dinshah Health Society
100 Dinshah Drive
Malaga, NJ 08328
(609) 692-4686
* Color and Light Therapy.

National Association of Holistic Aroma-therapists
P.O. Box 17622
Boulder, CO 80308-7622
(303) 447-9598

Spectrum Research Institute (Steven Halpern)
620 Taylor Way No. 14
Belmont, CA 94002
* Music

United Research, Inc.
P.O. Box 1146
Black Mountain, NC 28711
(704) 669-6845
* Prayer center & color healing

103

Nutrition

Flower Essence Society (Herbalism)
P.O. Box 459
Nevada City, CA 95959
(916) 265-9163

East West Foundation (Macrobiotic)
P.O. Box 850
Brookline, MA 02147

North American Vegetarian Society
P.O. Box 72
Dolgeville, NY 13329

Hippocrates Health Institute
25 Exeter Street
Boston, MA 02116
(617) 267-9525

Preventive Medicine

American Academy of Medical Preventics
2811 L Street
Sacramento, CA 95816
(916) 456-3378

Integral Health Services
245 School Street
Putnam, CT 06260
(203) 928-7729

International Academy of Preventive Medicine
10409 Town & Country Way, Suite 200
Houston, TX 77024
(713) 468-7851

Linus Pauling Institute of Science & Medicine
2700 Sand Hill Road
Menlo Park, CA 94025
(415) 854-0843

Medical Self-Care
Box 717
Inverness, CA 94937
(415) 663-8462

American Association of Professional Hypnotherapists
P.O. Box 29
Boones Mill, VA 24065
(703) 334-3035

Books

THE ACUPRESSURE FACELIFT by Lindsay Wagner and Robert M. Klein. Wagner/ Wagner/Ball Productions, Inc. Published by Prentice Hall Press.

ACUPRESSURE WAY OF HEALTH: JIN SHIN DO by Iona Marsaa Teeguarden. Tokyo Japan Publications, 1978, distributed by Harper & Row.

ACUPUNCTURE WITHOUT NEEDLES by J.V. Cerney, D.C., A.B., D.M., D.P.M., Parker Publishing Company.

ACU-YOGA--THE ACUPRESSURE STRESS MANAGEMENT BOOK by Michael Reed Gach. Tokyo Japan publications, 1981.

THE BACH FLOWER REMEDIES including three books in one volume (**HEAL THY-SELF** and **THE TWELVE HEALERS** by Edward Bach, M.D. and **THE BACH REM-EDIES REPERTORY** by F.J. Wheeler, M.D. Keats publishing, Inc., New Canaan, CT, 1979.

THE BAREFOOT DOCTOR'S MANUAL (The American translation of the Official Chinese Paramedical Manual) Philadelphia, PA., Running Press, 1977.

THE BODY ELECTRIC--ELECTROMAGNE-TISM AND THE FOUNDATION OF LIFE by Robert O.Becker & Gary Seldon. New York: William Morrow & Company, Inc., 1985.

THE BOOK OF INTERNAL EXERCISES by Stephen T. Chang. San Francisco: Strawberry Hill Press, 1978.

COLOR & MUSIC IN THE NEW AGE by Corrine Heline. New Age Press.

COLOR THERAPY by R.B. Amber. Calcutta, India, 1964.

THE COMPLETE BOOK OF ACUPUNC-TURE by Stephen T. Chang. Millbrae, CA: Celestial Arts, 1976.

CRANIOSACRAL THERAPY by John E. Upledger, D.O., F.A.A.O. and Jon D. Vredevoogd, M.F.A. Eastland Press, Seattle.

DO IT YOURSELF SHIATSU by W. Ohashi. New York: E.P. Dutton & Company, 1976.

THE EDGAR CAYCE HANDBOOK FOR HEALTH THROUGH DRUGLESS THERAPY (based on Dr. Harold J. Reilly's 45 years work with the Cayce readings) by Harold J. Reilly P.Ph.T., D.S., and Ruth Hagy Brod. MacMillan Publishing Company, Inc., New York.

FASTING: THE ULTIMATE DIET by Allan Coatt. New York: Bantam Books, 1975.

GETTING WELL AGAIN: A STEP-BY-STEP, SELF-HELP GUIDE TO OVERCOMING CANCER FOR PATIENTS & THEIR FAMILIES by Carl O. Simonton, Stephanie Mathews-Simonton, and James Creighton. Los Angeles: J.P. Tarcher, 1978.

HANDBOOK OF UNUSUAL & UNORTHO-DOX HEALING METHODS by J.V. Cerney, D.C., A.B., D.M., D.P.M. Parker Publishing Company.

HEALING MASSAGE TECHNIQUES: HO-LISTIC, CLASSIC AND EMERGING METHODS by Frances Tappan. Norwalk, CT: Appleton & Lang, 1988.

HEALING & REGENERATION THROUGH MUSIC by Corrine Heline. New Age Press.

HEALTH BUILDING by Dr. Randolph Stone, D.O., D.C. CRCS Publications: P.O. Box 1460, Sebastopol, CA 95473.

HELPING YOURSELF WITH FOOT RE-FLEXOLOGY by Mildred Carter. Parker Publishing Company, Inc., New York, 1977.

HIGH TECH TOUCH: ACUPRESSURE IN THE SCHOOLS by Jeanne St. John. Academic Therapy Publications, 20 Commercial Blvd., Navato, CA 94947-6191.

HOMEOPATHY, MEDICINE OF THE NEW MAN by G. Vithoulkas. New York, Avon Books, 1971.

HOW TO MEDITATE, A GUIDE TO SELF-DISCOVERY by Lawrence LeShan. Ballantine, 1975.

INNER BRIDGES, A GUIDE TO ENERGY MOVEMENT & BODY STRUCTURE by Fritz Smith, M.D. Atlanta, GA: Humanics Limited, 1990.

INTEGRAL THERAPY: AN APPROACH TO BODY, MIND, EMOTIONS & SOUL by Aminah Raheem. Los Angeles, CA: Stomel Publishing, 1986.

THE JOY OF FEELING: BODYMIND ACUPRESSURE by Iona Marsaa Teeguarden, P.O. Box 1800, Idyllwild, CA 92349.

KINESIOLOGY AND APPLIED ANATOMY by Philip J. Rasch. Philadelphia, PA: Lea & Bebiger, 1989.

THE MOOSEWOOD COOKBOOK by Mollie Katzen. Ten Speed Press, P.O. Box 7123N, Berkeley, CA 94707.

THE NEW AEROBICS by Kenneth H. Cooper. New York: M. Evans and Company, 1970.

POLARITY THERAPY, VOLUME ONE & POLARITY THERAPY, VOLUME TWO by Dr. Randolph Stone, D.C., D.O. CRCS Publications, P.O. Box 1460, Sebastopol, CA 95472.

PROCESS ACUPRESSURE by Aminah Raheem, Ph.D., P.O. Box 1727, Capitola, CA 95010.

RELAX WITH SELF-THERAP/EASE by Bonnie Pendleton and Betty Mehling. Englewood Cliffs, NJ: Prentice-Hall, 1984.

SOUL RETURN: INTEGRATING BODY, PSYCHE AND SPIRIT by Aminah Raheem, Ph.D. P.O. Box 1727, Capitola, CA 95010.

THE NEXT STEP...Re-Unification with the Presence of God Within our Hearts by Patricia Diane Cota-Robles. Order from: The New Age Study of Humanity's Purpose, Inc . P. O. Box 41883, Tucson, Arizona 85717

TOUCHING: THE HUMAN SIGNIFICANCE OF SKIN by Ashley Montagu. New York: Harper & Row, 1986.

VEGETARIAN TIMES COOKBOOK available from: Vegetarian Times Bookshelf, P.O. Box 570, Oak Park, IL 60303.

Tapes

CREATIVE IMAGERY by Audrey Murr Copeland with music by Mike Rowland. Audrey says: "Thought is creative. Let the creative mind create. Visualization and relaxation gets you in touch with your own power." Each cassette is $12 plus $2 shipping and handling. Order from: NFSHA, P.O. Box 2022, Mt. Pleasant, SC 29465.

JIM GOURE TAPES – EFFECTIVE PRAYER; THE NEW LIFE; BEING DIVINE, and many, many more. Write to: United Research, P.O. Box 1146, Black Mountain, NC 28711 or call (704) 669-6845. They also will give you information on conferences and intensives scheduled.

LIMITLESS PHYSICAL PERFECTION— PART ONE & PART TWO by Patricia Diane Cota-Robles. Order from: The New Age Study of Humanity's Purpose, Inc., P.O. Box 41883, Tucson, Arizona 85717.

* Many other tapes available from them. Ask for a listing.

Alkalinity-Acidity of Foods

When foods are eaten they are oxidized in the body, which results in the formation of a residue or ash. In this residue, if the minerals sodium, potassium, calcium, and magnesium predominate over sulfur, phosphorus, chlorine, and uncombusted organic acid radicals, they are designated as alkaline ash foods. The converse of this is true for foods designated as acid ash.

Numerical values of alkalinity or acidity are determined in long, painstaking, analytical laboratory work. The concentrations of the various elements are determined separately and then computed in terms of equivalents. The excess of one group of minerals over the other is expressed as cubic centimeters of normal acid or base (alkaline) per 100 grams of edible food. The values obtained are called degrees of acidity or alkalinity.

Most Alkaline Reaction

43.7 Fig, dried	8.5 Lemon with peel	6.7 Sweet Potato
41.6 Lima bean, dried	8.5 Coconut meat, dry	6.6 Apricot, fresh
36.6 Apricot, dried	8.5 Rutabaga	6.5 Turnip
25.3 Raisin	8.4 Onion	6.4 Grapefruit
20.4 Swiss chard	8.3 Tomato, ripe	6.2 Nectarine
20.3 Prune, dried	8.2 Peach, fresh	6.2 Cabbage
17.5 Dandelion greens	8.2 Plum	6.0 Banana
16.4 Soybean sprouts	8.1 Celery	6.0 Coconut, fresh
15.8 Spinach	8.1 Watercress	5.8 Pineapple
15.0 Taro tubers	7.7 Blackberry	5.7 Raspberry
14.2 Cucumber	7.7 Guava	5.7 Tangerine
14.0 Lima bean, fresh	7.7 Lemon, no peel	5.5 Gooseberry
13.5 Almond	7.7 Bamboo shoots	5.0 Mango
12.1 Peach, dried	7.7 Iceberg lettuce	4.9 Quince
11.1 Beet	7.5 Cantaloupe	4.9 Mushroom
10.7 Avocado	7.5 Coconut milk	4.8 Sapodilla
10.5 Kale	7.4 Loganberry	4.8 Snap bean
10.4 Chive	7.4 Pea, dried	4.8 Radish
10.2 Carrot	7.3 Sweet cherry	4.5 Orange juice
10.2 Rhubarb	7.3 Leek	4.5 Eggplant
9.9 Endive (escarole)	7.2 Potato	4.5 Okra
9.6 Date	7.1 Orange	4.3 Brussels spr.

9.1 Chestnut	7.0 Lettuce, cos	4.2 Broccoli
8.6 Parsnip	6.9 Prickly pear	4.2 Horseradish
		4.1 Sour cherry
		4.0 Lemon juice
		3.9 Red cabbage
		3.5 Pomegranate
		3.4 Pear, fresh
		3.2 Cauliflower
		3.2 Chicory
		3.2 Pumpkin
		2.8 Winter squash
		2.7 Grapes
		2.7 Savoy cabbage
		2.5 Strawberry
		2.2 Apple
		2.2 Watermelon
		1.8 Sweet corn
		1.3 Peas, fresh
		.1 Olive oil (Neutral)

Most Acid Reaction

11.3 Rye grain	8.5 English walnut	3.2 Brazil nut
10.9 Wheat grain	7.8 White rice	2.1 Filberts
10.6 Peanuts	4.3 White bean, dried	1.4 Blueberry
10.5 Lentils	4.3 Artichoke, globe	.8 Sorghum grain
10.3 Jerusalem artichoke	3.8 Olive, green pickled	.2 Water chestnut, Chinese
		.1 Asparagus

Author's Biography

The Rev. Dr. Angela Plum has been studying spiritual and holistic health techniques since a "death experience" triggered her search in 1950. She has worked with development groups since 1969, was a member of retreat committees for Spiritual Frontiers Fellowship, and was a founder, board member, and chairperson of conferences for Life Spectrums. She is a graduate of the following courses:

Integrated Awareness (Connie Newton)

Psychic Diagnosis (Connie Newton)

Spiritual Healing (National Federation, England)

Reiki I (Takata); Reiki II (Ethel Lombardi)

MariEl (Ethel Lombardi)

Psychic Surgery (Dr. Raymond Reed)

Polarity Therapy (Dr. Randolph Stone).
She became a Registered Polarity Practitioner in 1991.

Zero Balancing (structural acupressure,
Fritz Smith, M.D.) She was certified
by Dr. Fritz Smith in 1985.

Craniosacral Therapy (Franklyn Sills, England)

Process-Oriented Acupressure (Aminah
Raheem, Ph.D.)

Miraculous Healing (Dr. Wayne Chenault)

Angela has taught workshops in Auras,
Psychometry, Meditation, Psychic Development, Using the Powers of the Mind, and
various methods of Healing. She is an ordained Interfaith Minister with a Doctor of
Ministry degree from The International College of Spiritual and Psychic Sciences from
Montreal, Quebec, Canada, and a Doctor of
Philosophy in Therapeutic Counselling
(Ph.D.) from the Open International University of Sri Lanka. She is the author of several
books. The first one, **AN INTERFAITH
MINISTER'S MANUAL**, was published by
WorldComm® in March 1993. This book,
**ALTERNATE HEALING METHODS: AN
OVERVIEW,** is her attempt to give information on the various methods of alternate healing that are available.

The Rev. Dr. Plum has a private practice, teaches workshops, and provides ministerial services. She has been given an initiation technique which cuts the etheric ties to the past and heals the etheric body. For further information contact:

REV. DR. ANGELA PLUM, Ph.D.
5 PINEY VIEW ESTATES
MARSHALL, NC 28753
(704) 683-1737

Workshops Available:

Mastery, or The Path to Wholeness Workshop

Copyright 1993
By Rev. Dr. Angela Plum

In this workshop you will learn how to contact the Divinity within you and create a positive lifestyle. You will learn positive thinking, visualization, breathing techniques, exercises to balance your energies, and polarity hand contacts to open up blocked energy to establish the proper flow and alignment of the Life-force in the body.

We will end with an initiation ceremony which was given to me when I prayed for a method of healing the etheric body. The words given to me were that it would release ties to past relationships, addictions, patterns of behavior, and belief systems, both known and unknown, back through all life experiences to the beginning of time. The infusions of Light used in the technique also activate the radiant atoms in the DNA to begin the building of the radiant body which is our next step in evolution. Thus, you will be in charge of creating your own environment and be able to go within for your own guidance.

This workshop can be compressed into a 1-Day or 2-Day workshop or expanded to a 5-Day workshop suitable to a week's conference format. The fee for the workshop will depend on the time covered and the cost of travel and overhead.

For detailed information, contact:

REV. DR. ANGELA PLUM
5 PINEY VIEW ESTATES
MARSHALL, NC 28753
(704) 683-1737

Rainbow Bridge Meditation Techniques

Workshop
by Rev. Dr. Angela Plum

I. History of Rainbow Bridge

II. How to Build the Bridge

III. Buddhic Columns (How to remove negativity)

IV. Pranic Triangle (To energize the body)

V. Heart Center Meditation (How to activate your quiescent solar plexus center and telepathic interplay)

VI. Clearing Techniques (Eliminate thought-forms and emotions of ancient and low vibration)

1. Retrogression

2. Violet flame

3. RB Phase II line work

VII. "As If" Technique (For changing thinking and action)

* These techniques can be taught as: Classes for 8 weeks; as 5 2-hour classes or as a 2-day workshop with Basic (items I, II, III, IV) for 1st day and Advanced (items V, VI, VII) for the 2nd day; or Basic RB can be taught as a 6-hour workshop alone and the same for the Advanced RB.

FOR INFORMATION CONTACT:

REV. DR. ANGELA PLUM
5 PINEY VIEW ESTATES
MARSHALL, NC 28753
(704) 683-1737

1-Day Workshop

by Rev. Dr. Angela Plum

OVERVIEW OF POLARITY THERAPY

In this workshop you will learn what Polarity Therapy is, how energy moves in the body, some exercises to keep that energy balanced, and see a demonstration of Polarity for specific problems.

WORKSHOP CONTENT

I. Description of the Principles and Aspects

II. How Energy Flows in the Body

III. Dr. Stone's Exercises

IV. Use of the Hands

    A. Kinds of Contact

    B. Types of Touch

    C. Polarity of Fingers & Toes

V. Specific Hand Contacts For:

    A. Headaches

    B. Tension in Shoulders

    C. Digestion & Circulation

    D. Respiration

    E. Colon Problems

FOR INFORMATION CONTACT:

REV. DR. ANGELA PLUM, RPP
5 PINEY VIEW ESTATES
MARSHALL, NC 28753
(704) 683-1737

Basic Polarity Therapy

2-Day Workshop
by Rev. Dr. Angela Plum

This a beginning Polarity Therapy workshop showing you how to use these dynamic techniques to balance energies. You will learn the polarity of the fingers and toes, the specific positions on the body relating to the major body systems and practice doing the hand contacts to balance the energies. If you already practice any kind of body work, this will give you a valuable additional tool. Otherwise, you may want to study to be a Polarity Therapist or use what you learn to help self and family.

DAY 1

I. Background

II. Principles & Aspects

III. Polarity Exercises

IV. The Body Reflected in:

    A. Face

    B. Ears

    C. Thumbs

    D. Hands

    E. Feet

V. How Energy Flows in the Body

VI. Using the Hands

    A. Polarity of Fingers & Toes

    B. Kinds of Contact

    C. Types of Touch

    D. Differences in Hands

DAY 2

I. Major Body Systems

    A. Fire - Heart & Digestion

    B. Air - Respiration & part of circulation

    C. Water - Body fluids, lympathics, reproductive organs

    D. Earth - Elimination

II. Specific Treatments

III. Ways to Keep Energy Balanced

    A. Natural positions

    B. Fast & easy holds

    C. Polarity Circle

FOR INFORMATION CONTACT:

REV. DR. ANGELA PLUM, RPP
(704) 683-1737

A new aid for interfaith ministers:

AN INTERFAITH MINISTER'S MANUAL

An Interfaith Minister's Manual

by Reverend Dr. Angela Plum

Here is a new book for practicing interfaith ministers and anyone interested in the beliefs and rituals of the world's major religions. *An Interfaith Minister's Manual* is a book gathering ceremonies from most of the world's major religions into one volume that features information on the rituals and ceremonies of Catholic, Universal Spiritualist, Buddhist, Jewish, and other faiths.

First, there are listings of Jewish, Islamic, Buddhist, and Christian feast days, and then a glossary of religious symbols and what they mean to different faiths. Then follow complete scripts for performing baptisms, confirmations, marriages, anointing of the sick, and ordination of ministers, particularly from Universal Spiritualist and Catholic faiths. Also, scripts for candlelighting services and funerals.

The chapters on blessings and meditations features rituals for individual or group meditation, and blessings and exorcisms of buildings, beings, and objects. And last, a collection of various prayers.

6" x 9 1/2," 320 pages.
Hardback   ISBN 1-56664-026-1.........$25.00

Mail orders to: Rev. Dr. Angela Plum
5 Piney View Estates,
Marshall, N.C. 28753
(704) 683-1737

Enclose payment in U.S. dollars.

25% discount for orders of 5 books or more.
Add $2.00 shipping and handling for one item, $2.50 for two, and $3.50 for each shipment of five.
N.C. residents add 6% sales tax.